Ostriches
and Other Flightless Birds

Ostriches
and Other Flightless Birds

by Caroline Arnold/photographs by Richard R. Hewett

A Carolrhoda Nature Watch Book

Carolrhoda Books, Inc./Minneapolis

Thanks to Dr. Bonita Eliason,
Natural Resource Specialist,
Department of Natural Resources,
for her assistance with this book.

Additional photographs courtesy of: p. 42
(top and bottom), the New Zealand Consulate;
p. 43, Arthur Arnold

LIBRARY OF CONGRESS CATALOGING-IN-PUBLICATION DATA

Arnold, Caroline.
   Ostriches and other flightless birds / by Caroline Arnold;
photographs by Richard R. Hewett.
      p.   cm.
   "A Carolrhoda nature watch book."
   Includes index.
   Summary: An introduction to the physical characteristics, habits,
and natural environment of ostriches and a variety of other birds
that do not fly including the rhea, emu, cassowary, kiwi, and
tinamou.
   ISBN 0-87614-377-X (lib. bdg.)
   1. Ostriches—Juvenile literature. 2. Birds—Juvenile literature.
[1. Ostriches. 2. Birds.] I. Hewett, Richard, ill. II. Title.
QL696.S9A76   1990
598'.5—dc19   89-820
                                                   CIP
                                                   AC

Manufactured in the United States of America

1 2 3 4 5 6 7 8 9 10 99 98 97 96 95 94 93 92 91 90

We are grateful to all the people who helped us on this project. In particular, we would like to thank the staff of Wildlife Safari in Winston, Oregon; the Los Angeles Zoo, the San Francisco Zoo, and the Los Angeles County Museum of Natural History in California; and the Woodland Park Zoo in Seattle, Washington, for helping us obtain the information for this book and for the opportunity to take photographs. We also give special thanks to Phil and Margaret Sargent of the San Diego Ostrich Ranch in Escondido, California, for sharing their time and knowledge with us and for allowing us to get to know their ostriches.

Stepping forward on long, sturdy legs, a young ostrich begins to run. His head, perched on a tall, slender neck, turns as he scans the landscape ahead, and his wings flap like large sails.

Despite their feather-covered bodies, ostriches do not seem much like what we think of as birds. Most birds are small tree-dwelling animals that can fly. Ostriches, however, are enormous, and their wings are not strong enough to lift their heavy bodies off the ground.

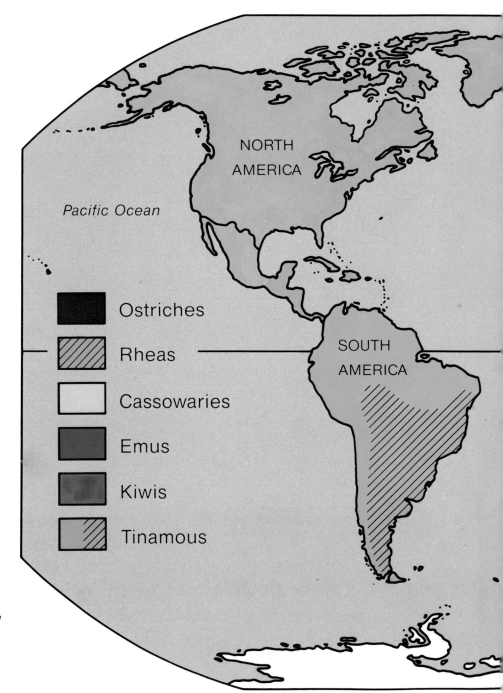

World map showing where ostriches and other flightless birds live.

Ostriches are native to the dry, open plains of northern, eastern, and southern Africa, where they mingle with other grassland animals, such as giraffes and zebras. They used to live on the Arabian Peninsula, until the last ones were killed by hunters in the 1940s. Much of the land in Africa has been developed for raising crops and domestic animals. Because the number of ostriches there has decreased so dramatically, most African countries now have laws that prohibit the hunting of ostriches.

NORTH AMERICA

Pacific Ocean

Ostriches

Rheas

Cassowaries

Emus

Kiwis

Tinamous

SOUTH AMERICA

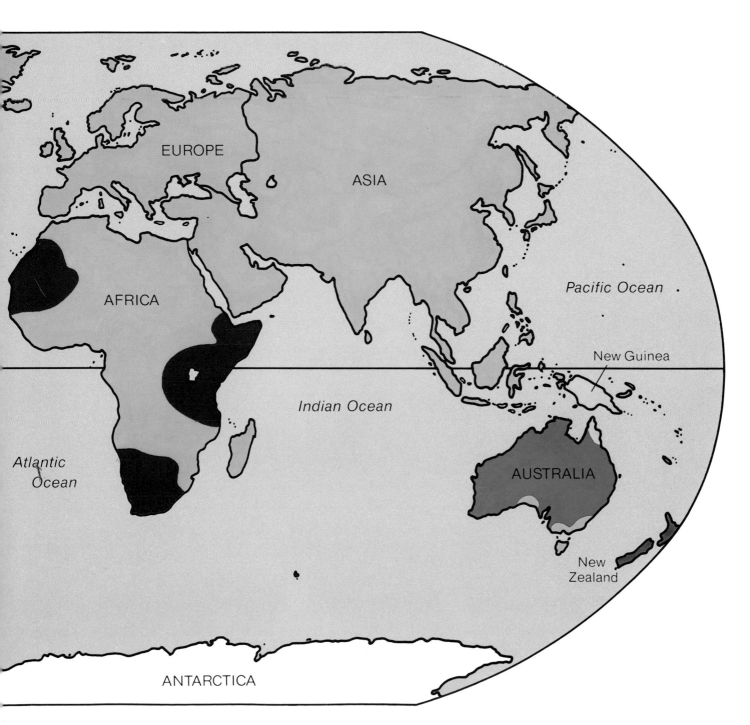

EUROPE

ASIA

AFRICA

Pacific Ocean

New Guinea

Indian Ocean

Atlantic
Ocean

AUSTRALIA

New
Zealand

ANTARCTICA

People have been fascinated by ostriches for thousands of years. Ancient rock paintings show that these large birds were once an important food for native Africans. In ancient Egypt, China, and Greece, people used ostrich eggshells as drinking cups and storage containers. During the Middle Ages, knights wore ostrich plumes in their armor, and at the beginning of the 1900s, ostrich feathers were fashionable on ladies' hats. Today, ostrich feathers are used in fashion and also in industry, where they are sometimes used to clean machinery.

Until the mid-1800s, ostrich feathers had always been collected from wild birds. Around 1850, however, the demand for ostrich feathers was so great that raising ostriches in captivity became profitable. Ostrich farms were established in many parts of the world, including Australia, Italy, Germany, South Africa, and the United States. In Australia, some of the ostriches escaped from the farms and adapted to life in the wild. Even today, an occasional wild ostrich can be seen there.

In the United States, ostrich ranches were located in Arizona, Florida, and California—places where the climate is warm year-round. They raised ostriches mainly to produce feathers, but ostrich ranches also produced meat, leather, and eggs. Sometimes ostriches were trained to race or to carry riders. In the 1920s, when ostrich feathers were no longer fashionable, many of these ranches went out of business. Most of those that remained were in South Africa. Recently, however, a new interest in raising ostriches has developed in the United States and elsewhere, because laws prohibit the export of ostrich products from South Africa.

Ostriches **molt**, or lose their feathers, once a year. On ostrich ranches, the feathers are cut off before the molting period to prevent them from becoming dirty or damaged. This is a painless process similar to getting a haircut. New feathers grow in quickly to replace the old ones.

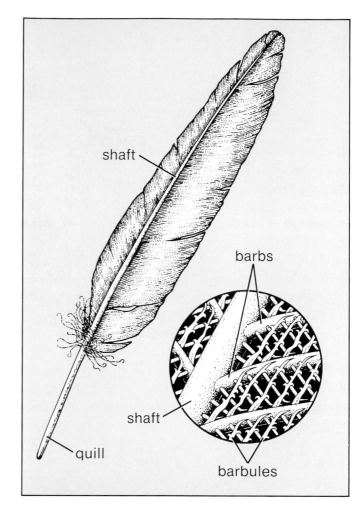

Each feather is formed around a central shaft. The lower bare part of the shaft is called the **quill**. Beyond the quill, on each side of the shaft, are tiny feathery strands called **barbs**. Most birds have barbs that are joined together with small hooks called **barbules**. They make the feathers appear smooth. Ostrich feathers are unusual because they do not have barbules. Instead, their feathers form softly flowing plumes. Another difference between ostrich feathers and those of most birds is their shape. The barbs of the feathers of most birds are shorter on one side of the shaft than on the other. Ostrich feathers have barbs of equal length. Because of its even balance, the ancient Egyptians used the ostrich's wing feather as a symbol of truth and justice.

Feathers protect birds by keeping them warm and dry. Ostriches keep their feathers clean and neat by pulling them through their beaks, a process called **preening**. The longest feathers on an ostrich are at the ends of the wings and tail. The body is covered with shorter, more densely packed feathers that act like a thick coat and help keep the ostrich warm when nights are cool. Preening also spreads body oil over the feathers. The body oil keeps rain from soaking the bird. The water is repelled by the oil and runs off the ostrich's back.

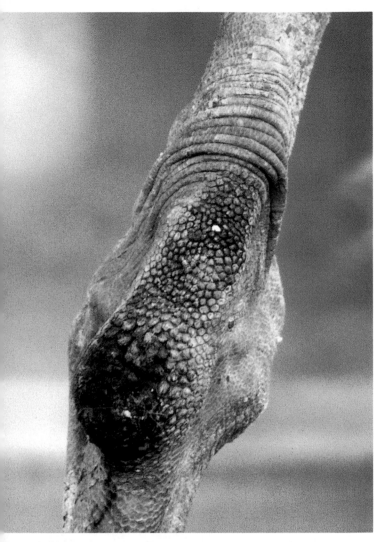

Birds first appeared on earth more than 200 million years ago during the age of dinosaurs. Scientists believe that birds developed from early reptiles, and today, similarities between these two animal groups remain: some members of both groups lay eggs, have some of the same kinds of bones in their skeletons, and are partially covered by scales. For instance, ostriches have flat reptile-like scales on their legs and feet.

The ostrich foot is unusual in that it has only two toes. All other birds have three or more toes on each foot. Each ostrich toe is long and ends in a clawlike nail, which helps the ostrich grip the ground when it runs. The foot is also used as a defense. If an ostrich is attacked, it kicks its feet forward and down using the sharp nails at the end of the toes to slash its foe. An ostrich may also try to defend itself by running toward an attacker and pecking it with its sharp beak.

One well-known myth about ostriches is that they bury their heads in the sand to avoid danger. When standing in long grass, an ostrich may appear to have its head below ground as it bends over to eat, but in fact, no one has ever seen an ostrich actually bury its head underground. In an effort to conceal themselves, young ostriches do sometimes lie down and stretch their necks flat along the ground, and adults sometimes stretch their necks flat on the ground when they're asleep or incubating eggs. Usually, though, ostriches prefer to run from danger.

Ostriches can run faster than any other two-legged animal and can accelerate to 40 mph (64 kph) in less than two seconds. Their legs reach out in long strides of up to 22 feet (6.7 m). Ostriches do not tire easily and can keep up a pace of 30 mph (48 kph) for 20 minutes or longer. While running, they hold their wings slightly out from their bodies. This may help the birds keep their balance and change direction quickly. From a distance, running ostriches appear to be skimming across the surface of the ground.

Sometimes when frightened, ostriches run in circles. Hunters often take advantage of this behavior and capture or kill ostriches while they are in this frightened state. Occasionally, a group of running ostriches suddenly stops, and the birds begin twirling like feathery ballerinas. No one knows why they do this.

In Africa, the chief enemies of ostriches are people and large wildcats, such as cheetahs and lions. Cheetahs, the fastest of all four-legged animals, have been seen chasing ostriches, jumping on their backs and killing them.

Ostriches can spot danger easily because of their height and excellent eyesight. Giraffes and elephants are the only animals on the African plain that are as tall as, or taller than, ostriches. From their high viewpoint, ostriches can spot danger in the distance and are often the first to see an approaching predator. A fleeing ostrich is a warning signal to other animals, such as gazelles and zebras, who also flee even though they cannot see the danger themselves.

18

The ostrich's eyes, which have a diameter of 2 inches (5 cm), are the largest eyes of any bird and are larger than those of any other land animal. The eyes are located on either side of the head, enabling the ostrich to see on both sides of its body at the same time. Each eye has a lid lined with long lashes that help protect it from dust and dirt. The **nictitating membrane**, a semitransparent flap of skin that acts like a second eyelid, closes upward and protects the eye while allowing the ostrich to see. The ostrich also has a good sense of hearing. Birds' ears have no outer covering and appear as small holes on either side of the head.

Ostriches often follow zebras and other grazing animals across the plain. As the hoofed animals move through the grass, they disturb insects and small animals that the ostriches can snatch up and eat. Ostriches are mainly **herbivores**, eating grass and small plants, but given the opportunity, they will eat insects and small reptiles. In captivity, ostriches are usually fed alfalfa hay, nutritional pellets, and a variety of fruits and vegetables.

Ostriches eat quickly, snatching morsels of food with their strong beaks. They have no teeth, so they swallow their food whole. While eating, ostriches also swallow small pebbles that mix with the food and help break it into smaller, more digestible pieces.

Like all animals, ostriches need water. In the grasslands where they live, the seasons alternate between rainy and dry weather, each lasting for several months. Ostriches can get much of the water they need from the food they eat. During the dry season, though, ostriches usually stay near water holes. At that time, they may join with other family groups of ostriches to form a large herd of 40 to 50 birds. Sometimes a herd has as many as 600 birds. Adult males and females may form separate groups, leaving young birds to flock together. When the rainy season returns, however, the herd splits into family groups again, and they move out across the plain. Breeding usually occurs during the rainy season, when there is plenty of food available.

Male ostrich

The ostrich is the largest living bird. An adult may stand 6 to 8 feet (1.8-2.4 m) tall and weigh between 200 and 300 pounds (90.7-136 kg). Although all ostriches are the same species and have the same scientific name, *Struthio camelus,* there are several subspecies within this group.

Female ostrich

All members of a **species** have similar characteristics and can breed with each other. Among the subspecies of ostriches, small differences in size, color, or feather formation exist. The most noticeable difference between the ostrich subspecies is skin color; some have red skin on their necks and legs, and some have blue necks and legs.

The male ostrich is sometimes referred to as a **cock** and the female as a **hen**. They are about the same size; the main difference in their appearance is the color of their feathers. Females are brownish gray, whereas males are black with white tips on their wings and tails. Ostriches usually live in family groups composed of one male and one to four females.

Adult ostriches can breed for the first time when they are three years old. Courtship begins when the female is ready to accept the male's advances. Then the male calls out with a loud booming roar to attract her attention. He puffs up his neck, stands very tall with his wings slightly raised, and struts around her. He may then flap his wings and chase the female. In the final stage of the male ostrich's mating dance, he drops to his knees and weaves his body back and forth while fully extending his wings. If the female accepts his courtship, she will sit on the ground and allow him to mate with her.

During the mating season, the male may court one or more females. A typical

family group is one male and two or three females. One of the females, usually the oldest, is the dominant, or **major**, female in the group. If two males are trying to attract the same female at the same time, there may be a fight. At first, the two males make hissing and booming noises at each other. Then they may chase each other and try to strike each other with their strong beaks.

After the courtship period, each male takes his hen or group of hens to the place he has selected for their nest. Ostriches do not build nests like many other birds do. Instead, the male simply scrapes a shallow hole in the dirt or sand.

The ostrich egg is white, slightly oval, and about 8 inches (20.3 cm) long. It weighs between 3 and 5 pounds (1.4-2.3 kg) and is the biggest egg in the world. Each ostrich egg is equal in size to about 24 chicken eggs. Yet no other bird lays such a small egg in proportion to its body size.

In her first breeding year, a female may lay only 4 or 5 eggs, but an older hen may lay as many as 15 eggs in the nest. The major female is always the first to lay eggs in the nest. If several females are laying in the same nest, there may be 30 or more eggs. It takes several weeks before all the females are finished laying their eggs. Usually, each female ostrich lays one egg every other day.

Ostriches share nest duty—both the male and the female **incubate** the eggs. The female sits on the eggs during the day, and the male sits at night. This protects the eggs and keeps them from becoming too hot or too cold. Ostrich eggs must be kept within a temperature range of 96° to 98° F (36°-37° C) for the chicks to develop. In a family group consisting of several females that have laid eggs, the major female is the one who incubates them. This female and the male will act as the parents to the chicks. The other females remain in the area and help look after the chicks after they hatch.

The parent birds use their feet and beaks to turn the eggs in the nest several times a day. This prevents the developing chick from becoming stuck to one side of the shell.

In a large nest, some of the eggs do not hatch. Ostriches cannot incubate more than 19 to 25 eggs at a time. Extra eggs are either pushed out of the nest or laid next to the nest and are not incubated, so they do not develop. An egg that has not been fertilized by the male during mating also will not develop. Sometimes the growing chick does not develop properly and dies. Other eggs may be eaten by hyenas or baboons if they can crack them open. Ostrich egg-shells are so tough that they do not break easily. Egyptian vultures drop rocks on ostrich eggs to crack them open, and lions have been known to play with the eggs as if they were large balls.

The eggs of ostriches in captivity (at zoos, wildlife parks, and ostrich ranches) are usually removed from the nest and placed in an incubator shortly after they have been laid. The incubator is a chamber that keeps the eggs at the same

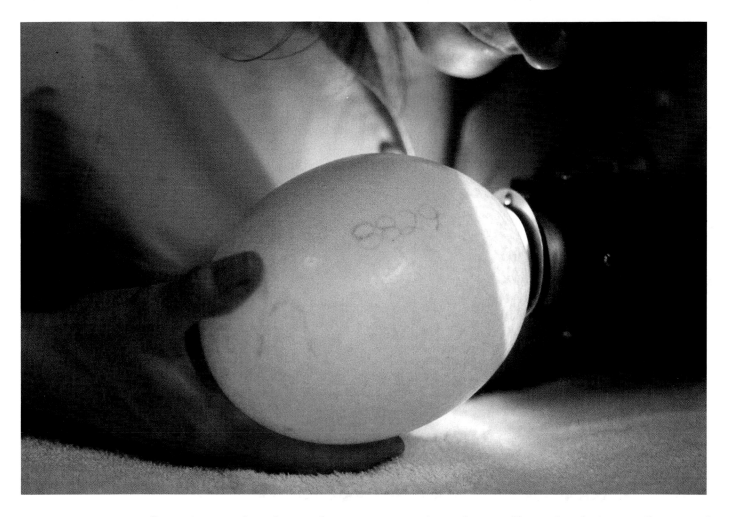

temperature and moisture levels as they would be in the nest. Each egg is labeled with a number that indicates when it was laid. In the incubator, the eggs are rotated regularly, just as they would be in the nest.

The development of the chick inside the egg can be monitored by a process called **candling**. In a dark room, the egg is held up to a light so a shadow of the interior can be seen through the shell. The dark portion of the egg contains the **yolk**, which is made up of nutrients, and the developing chick; and the light portion at the end of the shell is an air space. As the chick develops, it feeds on the yolk, so the air space becomes bigger. During incubation, moisture evaporates from the egg, so it becomes lighter. Therefore, the rate of the chick's development can be measured by weighing the egg. The lighter the egg, the closer it is to hatching.

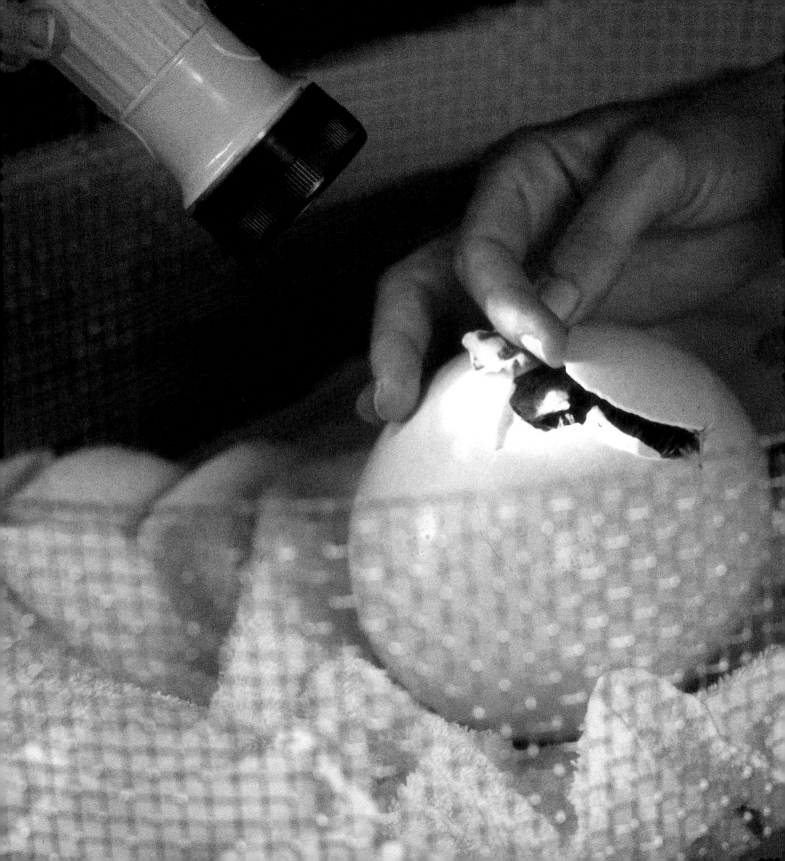

The eggs hatch about six weeks after they are laid. About one week before they are ready to hatch, the young chicks begin to make peeping sounds inside the eggs. The parent birds peep back at them. In this way, they learn to recognize each other's voices, even before hatching. The chicks can also hear each other, and this helps them hatch at about the same time. Even though the eggs were laid on different days, they have all been incubated for the same length of time. The chicks usually hatch within two to three days of each other.

The first sign of hatching is when the chick begins to **pip**, or break a small hole in the shell. The little chick must work hard to break its way out of the tough shell. From the beginning to the end, the hatching process may take up to two days.

At first, the newly hatched chick's feathers are wet and matted to its body. But after an hour or so, the feathers dry and become a soft, downy fluff. After hatching, the 1 foot (.3 m) tall, down-covered chick remains in the nest for about one day.

A newly hatched ostrich instinctively knows how to walk and how to peck for food; it does not need to be taught by its parents. Animals whose newborn can walk and find their own food are called **precocial**. Ostriches—among other birds, such as chickens and ducks—are precocial. Birds such as robins and sparrows, whose newborn must be fed by their parents, are called **altricial**. Altricial animals are less developed at the time of hatching or birth; they often have no body covering, and they cannot see or walk.

By the second or third day of life, ostrich chicks are rested and ready to explore the area around the nest. Their mottled brown feathers help them blend into their surroundings. In the wild, young chicks follow their parents as they move across the plain in search of food. Ostrich parents look after their chicks carefully. Even though they do not feed them, ostrich parents guard their chicks and protect them from predators. If danger is near, adult ostriches call to the chicks by making loud booming noises. The chicks either freeze where they are or run to hide under a parent's body. Sometimes the male ostrich tries to distract a predator by pretending to have a broken wing. By calling attention to himself, he hopes to lead the predator away from his family. Animals that prey on young chicks include wild dogs, hyenas, and large birds of prey.

The chicks grow at a rate of about 1 foot (.3 m) a month for the first six months. The juvenile birds get their adult feathers by their third year. Then they are ready to leave the family group and mate for the first time. An ostrich does not reach its full body size until it is 4 or 5 years old. The life span of an ostrich in the wild is about 40 years. In captivity, ostriches have been known to live for 80 years.

Ostriches and their relatives are among the most unusual birds alive today. Unlike every other kind of bird except the penguin, most of the ostrich's relatives cannot fly. Although scientists believe that these flightless birds are descended from ancient flying birds, the wings of present-day ostriches are useless for flight.

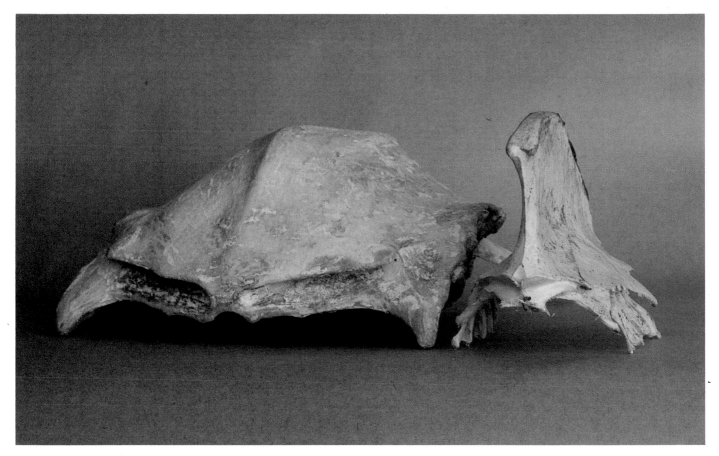

On the left is the gently rounded breastbone of the ostrich. On the right is the breastbone of a large flying bird, the Kori bustard. Notice the huge ridge.

Relatives of the ostrich include rheas, cassowaries, emus, kiwis, and tinamous. One way that these flightless birds differ from other birds is in their bone structure. Other kinds of birds have a breastbone with a large ridge that looks like the keel that runs along the bottom of a sailboat. The bird's strong flight muscles are attached to this part of the breastbone. Birds related to ostriches have breastbones without such a ridge. Their breastbones are gently curved, more like the bottom of a raft. The scientific name for ostriches and their relatives is *Ratitae*, or ratites, which is from the Latin word meaning raft. The bones of ratites are also much heavier than those of birds that fly—ratites have solid bones, whereas birds that fly have hollow bones. And birds that fly have a Y-shaped bone in front of the breastbone that we sometimes call the wishbone. Ratites do not have wishbones.

Male rhea courting two females

All of the ratites are found in the southern hemisphere. Rheas are native to South America and are similar to ostriches both in appearance and habits. They stand about 4 to 5 feet (1.2-1.5 m) tall, and, like ostriches, they live on the open plains, where they feed on a variety of plants, insects, and small animals. Although rheas were once hunted for their meat and beautiful feathers, they are now protected by law.

Rhea egg

Male rhea sitting on his nest

At breeding time in the spring, groups of five or six female rheas gather together and mate with a single male. They lay their large, dark green eggs in the nest that he has built. As many as 30 eggs may be laid in one nest. When the females finish laying their eggs, they disappear, leaving the male to incubate the eggs by himself. Only the male bird looks after the young rheas after they hatch. They grow quickly and within a few months are ready to be on their own.

The cassowary is a large, heavy bird that lives mainly in New Guinea. One species lives in northern Australia as well. The cassowary is about 4 to 5 feet (1.2-1.5 m) tall and is distinguished by a large bony growth on its head. This growth is called a **casque** and is taller on the female than on the male. The head, which is featherless, is usually bright blue. Cassowaries are shy forest creatures, usually moving about only at night.

The emu, on the other hand, is a daytime feeder and is adapted to the dry central plains of Australia. The emu is the national bird of Australia. In general, its habits resemble that of the ostrich or rhea. The emu is the second largest living bird, standing 5 to 6 feet (1.5-1.8 m) tall. Yet the emu's wings are so small that they are mere stubs compared to the wings of other birds. The emu's feathers, as well as those of the cassowary, are unusual in that two feathers grow out of each quill.

Top: *X-ray of a female kiwi with an egg inside. Kiwis lay the largest eggs in proportion to their body size.*

Bottom: *kiwi*

Tinamou

The remaining two ratites, the kiwi and the tinamou, are much smaller birds, each standing about 1 foot (.3 m) tall.

Kiwis are native to New Zealand. These strange-looking birds have no tails, useless tiny wings, and feathers that resemble coarse hairs. Kiwis are unusual in that their nostrils are at the end of their long, slender beaks. Kiwis are active at night, so people rarely see them in the wild. They walk around the forest, poking their beaks into the ground in search of earthworms, their favorite food. A female kiwi lays one egg that is nearly one-quarter her own body weight. No other bird lays such a large egg in proportion to its body size.

Tinamous are native to Central and South America and are the only ratites that can still fly. Unlike other ratites, the tinamou has a keeled breastbone. Other parts of the tinamou's skeleton resemble the ratites, so they have been placed in that group. There are 46 species of tinamous, and they are all ground-dwelling birds. They live in forests or bushy grasslands and eat a variety of plants and small insects.

Ratites are the oldest kind of bird alive today. The only kind of bird that is older, birds with teeth, became extinct long ago. Fossils show that ancestors of ratites lived 65 million years ago. In relatively recent times, several species of very large ratites have lived in Australia and New Zealand. A giant bird called *Genyornis,* which became extinct about 30,000 years ago, was hunted by the aborigines of Australia. Another huge bird, the moa, which used to live in New Zealand, became extinct only about 200 years ago. One species of moa was about 12 feet (3.7 m) tall and was the largest bird ever known.

Ostriches and other ratites, with their strange behaviors, flightlessness, and ancient heritage, belong to one of the most interesting animal groups. The ratites share many common characteristics, and although they are found on widely separated continents, their similarities suggest that the earth's land masses were once much closer together than they are now. By learning more about ostriches, rheas, cassowaries, emus, kiwis, and tinamous, we can learn about the earth today and imagine what life might have been like long ago.

GLOSSARY

altricial: being immature, helpless, and in need of care at the time of hatching or birth. *Compare with precocial.*

barbs: the side branches, or feathery strands, of the quill of a feather

barbules: the small hooks on barbs that are responsible for making a feather look either smooth or ruffled

candle: to examine the inside of an egg by holding it up to a light

casque: the large bony growth on the head of the cassowary

cock: a male bird

hen: a female bird

herbivore: an animal that eats only plants

incubate: to keep eggs at the right temperatures for the chicks to develop and hatch

major female: the dominant and usually the oldest female in an ostrich family

molt: to shed feathers periodically

nictitating membrane: a thin membrane that lies beneath the lower eyelid of many animals. This semi-transparent membrane protects the eye by closing up over it, while still allowing the animal to see.

pip: to break through the shell of an egg for the first time when hatching

precocial: able to walk and find food at the time of birth or hatching. *Compare with altricial.*

preen: to clean and smooth the feathers

quill: the hollow shaft of a feather

species: a group of animals and plants that share similar characteristics and can interbreed

yolk: the round, yellow portion of an egg that is made up of stored food used by the developing chick. The yolk is surrounded by a protective layer of fluid that is called the white of the egg.

INDEX

beaks, 27, 43; and defense, 14; and eating, 21
bone structure of flightless birds, 37, 43
breeding, 21, 24-25, 36

cassowaries, 37, 41
chicks, 33-34, 36, 39
courtship. *See* breeding

defenses, 14, 16, 18; and chicks, 34
distribution, of flightless birds, 8-9, 38, 41, 43; of ostrich ranches, 11

ears, 19
eating habits, of kiwis, 43; of ostriches, 20-21, 33, 34; of rheas, 38; of tinamous, 43
eggs, and candling, 29; and development of chicks, 27-29, 31; and hatching, 31, 33; in captivity, 29; of kiwis, 42, 43; of ostriches, 26-27; of rheas, 39; parts of, 29; shells of, 28; size of, 26, 42, 43
emus, 37, 41
enemies of ostriches, 18, 28, 34
eyesight of ostriches, 18-19

family groups, of ostriches, 21, 23, 25, 27; of rheas, 39
farms. *See* ranches
feathers, 36, 41, 43; and molting, 11; and preening, 13; diagram of, 12; in fashion, 10
feet of ostriches, 14, 27
fighting, 14, 25

herds, 21
history, of flightless birds, 36, 44; of ostriches, 10-11, 14
hunting, of ostriches, 8, 17; of rheas, 38

incubation, 16, 27-28. *See also* eggs

kiwis, 37, 43

laws, protecting ostriches, 8, 11; protecting rheas, 38
life span of ostriches, 36

mating. *See* breeding
mating dance, 24

nests, 25; and number of eggs, 26, 39. *See also* eggs
nictitating membrane, 19

ranches, 10-11
ratite, definition of, 37
rheas, 37, 38-39
running and ostriches, 7, 14, 16-17, 18

scientific classification, 22, 23
size, of cassowaries, 41; of emus, 41; of kiwi eggs, 43: of kiwis, 43; of ostrich eggs, 26; of ostriches, 18, 22-23, 33, 36; of rheas, 38; of tinamous, 43
speed of ostriches, 17

tinamous, 37; and ability to fly, 43

wings, 36; of emus, 41; of cassowaries, 41; of kiwis, 43; of ostriches, 17, 24

ABOUT THE AUTHOR

Caroline Arnold is the author of numerous widely acclaimed books for young readers, including the Carolrhoda Nature Watch titles *Saving the Peregrine Falcon, A Walk on the Great Barrier Reef,* and *Tule Elk*. Ms. Arnold is also an instructor in the UCLA Extension Writers' Program. She lives in Los Angeles with her husband and their two children.

ABOUT THE PHOTOGRAPHER

Richard R. Hewett graduated from the Art Center School of Design, in California, with a major in photojournalism. He has illustrated more than 30 children's books and collaborated with Caroline Arnold on the Carolrhoda Nature Watch titles *Saving the Peregrine Falcon* and *Tule Elk*. He lives in Los Angeles with his wife.